REFUGEE

poems by

Erika Michael

Finishing Line Press
Georgetown, Kentucky

REFUGEE

Copyright © 2025 by Erika Michael
ISBN 979-8-89990-237-6 First Edition
All rights reserved under International and Pan-American Copyright Conventions. No part of this book may be reproduced in any manner whatsoever without written permission from the publisher, except in the case of brief quotations embodied in critical articles and reviews.

Publisher: Leah Huete de Maines
Editor: Christen Kincaid
Cover Art: Samuel Guttmann
Author Photo: Isabelle Quinn
Cover Design: Elizabeth Maines McCleavy

Order online: www.finishinglinepress.com
also available on amazon.com

Author inquiries and mail orders:
Finishing Line Press
PO Box 1626
Georgetown, Kentucky 40324
USA

Contents

To Parents Fleeing The War Zone With A Child 1

sweeping the fragments

This Mental Game 5
Random Access Memory 6
Anschluss, Vienna, March 12, 1938 7
Tits For Fritz 8
Tens Of Thousands Hollered Heil 9
Augarten 10
Dirndl / Lederhosen 11
Rudolfinerhaus, Döbling 12
Risings 13
The Officer 14
Gut Holes 15
Smoke Gets In Your Lungs 16
In A Blue Dress 17
Wheels 18
My Grandfather The Watchmaker Came And Went 19
The Day We Left 20
SS Rex, Genoa To NY 21
What Happened To Jeki? Or Dog As Metaphor Of War 22

Amerika / America

New Soil 25
Erika, Erika, Wir Fahren Nach Amerika 26
A Bowel Of Silence 27
Goulash 28
Malakoff Torte 29
Maybe He Sold Both 30
Needletrades 31
Tannersville 32
Radetzky March 33
Last Boat To Havana 34
Grandfather's Seder 35

The Wandering 36
Song Sung To Omama–*Kommt Ein Vogel Geflogen*. 38
Beds 40
Reflections 41

epigenetic grit—"it's in my bones"

Photo Op 45
Luke Bow And Me, 1943 46
Éclair's 47
It's The Art 48
It's In My Bones—Ta Ram Pa Pa
I Love To Waltz With My Mama 49
Ich Kann Die Füss Net Schleppen 50
Epigenetics 51
Cousin Frank 52
Der Schlag Soll Sie Treffen 53
Tale From The Vienna Woods 54
History Lesson For Kids 56
Passing On My Keys 57
My Name Is Avrash 58

Acknowledgments 60
The Object Of These Poems 61
Gratitude 62

*to the memory of
my parents, Frances Goodman and Samuel Guttmann,
my grandparents, Paula and Hermann Wenig,
for all those who barely made it out—
and for those who didn't*

TO PARENTS FLEEING THE WAR ZONE WITH A CHILD

Bear your life on your back like
a snail, in the cells of your gut
silently piled, chronicles hidden
inside your head. We need you

to quarry roots from that cerebral
flower bed. Show us your paint-
flaked wagon by the backyard
gate—home's not yours to slice

out of our story for the bile of war.
Consider your kaleidoscope—
the cache of images stashed
within the gyri and sulci massed

and folded in that wizened shell,
fading pictures caught in milder
winds or in the sting of alien ice.
Burnish memories as clear graffiti

on the pages of your shredded
book, engrave them on the husks
of progeny, re-collect each acorn
of the oak to plant in plush new

beds so that the young can dig
for mulch of mingled nutrients—
the scribbles of their coil, a chance
to mass the stuff that flickered

by their toddler eyes before they
left in tear-soaked woolies drenched
with kisses at a train, tangled skeins
wanting to be knit again—

faded wreckage of goodbye.
Say how war ground all the action
to a halt, the wedding feast and bridal
dress, picnics by the willow pond,

cherries in a crystal bowl,
burials and *Yiskor* prayer, words to
recollect the tremolo of emptiness.
Speak of how you wolfed your rage,

that tang of bittersweet, your hunger
to be rid of belly angst, the minor
notes spit up as shame. Describe it for
posterity. Talk about the seedlings,

where they sprouted, how your sun-
flowers spun 'round as rain pooled
in the rubble, strawberries in underbrush,
a drift of spores, the recipes, the chop

and dice of pungency, the waft of
banter—bubbling synesthesia of the
kitchen door. Tell about the light,
how it glinted on the handle of your

leaving, how the seeds you stow still
groan under the stones. Polish all the
tints and tones, hone them to a glitter,
sprinkle them with dendrite gist

so those too little to recall can utter
in my bones—I remember this.

sweeping fragments

THIS MENTAL GAME

From this brittle slideshow of my brain
I try to capture fragile scraps in flight,

to chronicle my hippocampal code lest
all the signals die, to cut through tangled

vines of angst—a mental game to set me
free, an unhinged zip-line to my infancy.

RANDOM ACCESS MEMORY

I'd like to split the flickers of a browned
out past from Vienna's underscrub of guilt
and shame, rout the demons of amnesiac
intent, grasp fragile shreds to disentangle

objects which my parents couldn't name,
thrum the wires of their barbs, loose their
grip on wounds of lives gone wrong—
with humble deference to broken tongues.

ANSCHLUSS
VIENNA, MARCH 12, 1938

I toddled with my parents to the *Prater*
for a horsey-ride around the *Ringlespiel*
to see the *Riesenrad*—the giant wheel
of Harry Lime renown built for the Jubilee,

dark shadows of its rolling pods and spider
cables spinning arcs above the strollers
in the park—while in the city core, its massive
counterpart, the *Stephansdom*, rang out

with bells of Moslem canonball. March 12,
1938, as boxcars rolled along Vienna's malls,
those carillons clanked hollow as they had
on Beethoven's deaf ears. That morning

in the slanting sun a sea of arms and chants
of *Heil* pealed out in swells against the
braying of a carousel. At the astrological
observatory near *Franz Josefs Kai* where

bathers drifted by those Danube banks of
whitewashed memory, a few recalled the stars
had dimmed because this brownish fog had
settled in. We gazed upon St Stephan's gables

glazed in hues by Klimt—two-hundred-thirty
thousand tiles in yellow, black and green—
a zig-zag poster of post-Axis pride set within
those steeples' bones with spires thrust like

Schiele fingers, calloused warts and grief inside.

TITS FOR FRITZ

Astonishing how charismatic leaders
spawn the fealty of followers—what
soldiers do to fuel libido in a cramped
machine. The tanks roll in upon decree—
feast your eyes on power—we will set you free!

The crooning of a throng—gray matter's
readiness like lightening-to-wire waiting
its release, the city gate's ajar, the marchers
muted by the growl of wheels on cobbles
in a cheer-dowsed street. Now cries of

Heil and tidal wave of arms with flowers
raining on the helmets of the troops
who swagger by—the *grab-me* screams
like Frank Sinatra fans in '42—a flash
of teeth, the wild-eyed revel of a so-called

Aryan race, the craze of giddy females
straddling a caravan of tanks, the Rosas,
Mitzis and Marias screeching to the randy
males, Günter, Horst or Fritz, a swelling
of delirium as girls unhook their bras

and boys behold a sea of tits.

TENS OF THOUSANDS HOLLERED *HEIL*

The day of *Anschluss* people in the street
went feral for the troops. You could see it

in their gargoyled eyes as puffed up soldiers
flaunted not-so-secret grins, knowing well

how this convoy to *Heldenplatz* would
end for folks like us of suspect ancestry.

Thousands *heiled* their asses off the day
the Fuhrer took the mic to whip that sea

of frothing Austrians into a loathing for
the Christ-killer next door, trope-doped

a mass of hollering disciples clustered round
that foul persona of a Lie now seared into

the psyche of his *Volk*. We'd lock ourselves
in smoke-steeped rooms and turn the lights

out when the sun went down as neighbors
disappeared from town.

AUGARTEN

On sunny days, we toddlers in
the *Augarten* from Jewish homes
came out with mamas, nannies,
doggies, buckets-full of toys—

We rode the carousel and licked
our ice cream from a crispy pastry
shell. Our parents gossiped on
the benches while we frolicked

in the sprinkler pond, too small
to see those playgrounds growing
emptier. How many left, I don't
recall. But now and then we'd

find a cap or my dog Jeki would
exhume a ball.

DIRNDL / LEDERHOSEN

There's a photo of my mother
twenty-five or so, leaning on
a garden fence—I may already
be alive in her. She's attired

in the timeless Alpine *Dirndl*—
foil to *Lederhosen* worn at popular
events where my parents went
to mix it up with fellow Austrians.

But when my papa's aquiline
profile occasioned über-friendly
drool—that *Dirndl* and those
Lederhosen didn't feel as cool.

RUDOLFINERHAUS, DÖBLING

The Catholic sisters of the Rudolfinerhaus
christened me, this new-born Döbling denizen,
into their faith and pinned an *Edelweiss* onto
my swaddling as they placed me in the arms
of my *Mama*. Yet still *Hakadosh Baruch Hu*

beamed through my eyes. So this *converso*
on the sly, soul saved before she knew souls
were a thing, went forth into the world of Klimt
and Strauss and trips to *Semmering* for Alpine
drift with parents who, as Austrians, were

keen on it, hiking in the Kaiser's hunting
ground with feathered cap and curly hound.
I was baptized once more into the lore
of Danube blue, my body firmly held by
my *papa*, who dipped me in a grayish river

flowing in three quarter time to Sieczyński's
kitchy dream, *Wien Wien Nur Du Allein*—
Vienna, city of my dreams. When suddenly
they crooned another song to me in pained
and melancholy voice: *Erika, Erika, Wir*

fahren nach Amerika! America—not some
Shangri-La—but Neverland, away from
home-no-longer where no Jew could touch
a toe to ground without the sound of boots,
and pounding in the gut, a fracture in the DNA—

no flowing water's strong enough to cleanse
the blot of Anschluss that consumed the *Volk*
who *heiled* bare-breasted in their zeal for
that misbegotten prodigal. When the strains
of *Edelweiss* are warbled by the *Lederhosen* set,

I think about the shouts of *Juden raus* and all
the well-intentioned folk at Rudolfinerhaus.

RISINGS

The feces of important steeds are
known as 'risings' for their equine
aromatic air, perhaps a waft of ancient
glory from some martial enterprise

engraved on stable walls or penned
by scribes in chronicles, a caviar
of horse manure spread to mulch
the garden plots of cultivated genera.

The horse had dumped upon the
cobbled road—that's ploppled down,
not risen, someone had to clean it up,
so when an SS officer on Ringstrasse

proclaimed that Uncle Martin has
the honor of the sweep and handing
him a broom declared—*this is for the Jew!*
Martin sniffed the wind and knew.

THE OFFICER

An attractive young woman, she was
lithe, arched eyebrows,
sitting there posed in a black dress with cigarette,
wavy blaze of blond hair—
a Vienna Marlene Dietrich replica meeting
the lens with sultry gaze.

Now cast into a role ill-suited to
illusions of allure, the endless scenes in half-lit
rooms tending a child,
the craze of sticking to those curfew rules
tacked on to kiosk walls
and post office vitrines—

the knocks that summoned Aunt Adele
to muster at the square
and Uncle Martin to clean out latrines.
Restrictions pressed—and sour marriage bore
into her soul. She saw herself under
the Linden trees

and heard the crunch of gravel on the ground,
the hurdy-gurdy of a carousel, nearby the *Riesenrad*—
that ferris wheel of world renown.
Wearing her silken summer skirt
and highest heels, she walked out of the door
her daughter by the hand,

her blond hair gleaming in the sun—
she breathed the air.
Now footsteps close behind—
a dazzling officer fell into step
and asked her name—
she laughed,

her face flushed as his features,
aquiline and clear
framed a brilliant smile when he bent near,
his green eyes radiating to the bone—
     lady—he advised her softly
take your kid and go on home.

GUT HOLES

Scientists describe Black Holes as *potholes
in eternity so massive that they swallow even
light*, like holes that sprouted in my infant

brain before I grew the teeth to chew that
gristle—*Judenrein*—annihilation of the Jews
cooked up in stewpots of a bully and his gang.

My gut stirs up a gnawing from the stuff
I swallowed as my folks hashed out where
Jews were massed or thugs convened while

we hunkered behind *Jugendstil* vitrines
to pass the months in fear of knocks. For one
year and a half I clutched a rag doll while

my parents smoked and the cuckoo messed
with hippocampal floaters in my head as we
marked time by Sabbath candle clots.

SMOKE GETS IN YOUR LUNGS

Before VE Day, Uncle Martin smoked cigars
at poker parties in our NY living room—the rest
did Camels, Lucky Strikes, no filter tips. They
sucked them neat and sat there betting, black-out
shades drawn while air-raid wardens hollered
lights out on the street in case some German Junkers
had slunk into clouds above Long Island Sound.

I smell the acrid air that clung around the room
and in the lobe of every lung, and hung below
the ceiling like the musty flatus of a ghost balloon.
Fibrosis, my doctor said, asking *do you smoke,
or have you ever smoked?* I thought about old
road trips with my folks—how my eyes stung,
how I heaved and choked. But there were those

years before when we were shut behind doors
bolted against SS, when my parents chain-smoked
packs of *Memphis*—fancy brand dangling off
nicotine-stained hands. Smoke mingled with
fear coiled around the pendants of our chandelier.

IN A BLUE DRESS

Whacking my way through fragments of
my long gone childhood—I pick at edges
of recall to mull how we were flung like
chum into infested waters—not Vienna's
deep creative streams, but tossed off

folly's trolley as though circling the 'Ring'
along with bulwarked troops of Ataturk.
We cowered behind shades drawn against
the glinting face of a town sold down the
Danube dimmed by slant-salutes of torch

groupies mirroring their murky ripples
in the sludge of a Great Lie—*word candy*—
tossed to the bedazzled by a hate-huckster
who mesmerized his *Volk* to cleanse them
pure as Wotan's mythic race. First came

whispers then came shouts, warped reality
and spin, boundaries breached and disbelief,
lives destroyed like flakes of glass and
there I went—in a blue dress—with papa
and mama on the Transalpine Express.

WHEELS

Time stopped for the watchmaker, my grandfather
that day in October '39 at the Vienna *Südbahnhoff*
when his breath fell on my face for our last good-bye.

A child of two, I carried his blue eyes across the Alps
on freighted rails—my papa's arms, my mama's gaze—
glazed when the request *your papers please* sprung out

the ticking of her heart, my eardrum coiled against
her chest, those documents by forgers whose expertise
decided within milliseconds whether we would hear

the clack of iron wheels from inside a compartment
looking out or watch them from beyond a platform gate.
I can't conjecture how my grandfather evaded all those

thugs in brown who later sauntered past his door, but
Hakadosh Baruch Hu returned him to me in a fourth-floor
New York walk-up, where once more I savored his

familiar breath. At a black worktable alive with springs
and wheels, I watched the watchmaker start time again—
arraying jewels from shattered things.

MY GRANDFATHER THE WATCHMAKER CAME AND WENT

These eyes, like his,
the dichroic color of blue marbles,
have witnessed razor wire
humming

in pines. And
bracken, in which all this
can be read
or discounted,

will show
the nurse log begets gentian among cabbage.
As I dig
for tracks in that wood

these ruminations
on appearing and leave-taking are
sprung with the clocked accuracy
of a stroke at midnight.

THE DAY WE LEFT

A cozy ride inside a polished first class
cubicle of wood and brass had cost our
family the last of what we had to spend,
verboten to bring money out—this was
the trip we'd feared but dreamt about.

My child-eyes took in village upon village
on the spinning scrim of Alps. We passed
our old vacation spot, Bolzano with its
apples, cows in fields, its steepled churches
guarding boneyard plots, ancient world

of red-tiled roofs with chimney pots.
Once out of Austria we transferred to the
train for Genoa to link up with the SS Rex,
our ocean liner to the USA, and stumbled
on a bakery displaying zeppole and

cannoli. We had no "dough" but just like
when *The Holy One Blessed Be He* gave
manna to the Israelites, my mama reached
into her purse—Behold! there were some
Groschen—overlooked by the authorities.

SS REX / GENOA TO NYC
OCTOBER 1939

Waltzing—treading water really—in that
gilded ballroom on a Turkish Kilim carpet,
patterns deep as ocean breakers, portholes

garlanded and gilt like mirrors of Versailles
reflecting airs of Neptune or Aquarius,
but strictly speaking—Noah. We partook

of briny morsels sauced by master chefs and
served on swells of linen in a stately dining
hall, with fragile flutes of liberty anticipating

New World shores aboard a vessel flying
Axis colors—free of Fascist sensibilities,
ploughing missile-studded waters with a crew

who'd ferried thirty-thousand Jews to liberty.

WHAT HAPPENED TO JEKI?
OR DOG AS METAPHOR OF WAR

Let slip the dogs of war, they cried,
and so the many-headed Cerberus
flew off the fist—the "dog handlers
of Dachau" on command unleashed
their hounds to tear the prisoners
to bits, the red-eyed pack enraged with
spittle trickled on their gums and lips.

My Jeki—not a terror, but a terrier,
old snapshots show his white coat,
curly with some darker spots. I don't
know whether they were gray or brown.
He liked his liver, Mama said, and let
me put my fingers down his gullet.
When the peaceful dogs were called

to lick the poison bone, they lingered
fleetingly to warm a pillow, fetch
a stick, and then those baffled canines
gnawed the marrow from a stone.
My mother had to bring our Jeki
to a camp for Jewish dogs. Did he feel
abandoned, wondering where he'd

gone astray. Of course, it wasn't he,
but we who'd gone away—the roving
Jews aboard that bloody omnibus.
She's bending to his ear, and while
I thought I heard a fraught *good dog*
it might be that she said—*good God*

Amerika / America

NEW SOIL

We rose at five to watch the fog
thin on the face of Liberty, wept
at the torch's glint and gazed at
the haze of harbor lights.

Bags packed and papers gripped
we waited for the feel of that last
leg braced by our grief, those first
steps on the glittering streets.

America's boulevards are paved
with tar (we knew), the rumored
gold, a proposition scratched on
sheepskin years ago.

We had full grasp of that double
sided coin, freedom & duty, and
digging in new soil with bootstrap
grit—we laid bare the gist of it.

ERIKA, ERIKA, WIR FAHREN NACH AMERIKA

A ditty sung to me still flickers in my brain
Erika, Erika, we're going to America...
where streets glint under blacktop poured
with pitch o' goin' places—years o' rockin'

all that screech and reverie on subway trains.
Then comes an old refrain from a forgotten
choir as *dirty Jew's* muttered by a gut/dumb
teen in this land o' the free as he throws

a pack of burning butts into our window
screen and sets my sister's crib on fire.
Grown now—hopes spun into cap n' gown,
our *Strudel's* 'pie' and *Apfelsaft* is 'juice,'

we roast a turkey on Thanksgiving Day,
its waft and crackle's our golden goose.

A BOWEL OF SILENCE

I'd heard my mama's fond recall of
old romantic flings and love of operetta,
longing for *Kaffee* and *Sachertorte*.
In the end, her lips were clenched

on bitter coin—fraught with sour
disillusion as the neighbors shrank
before the shredded weavings of her
fabric, patterns of cacophony as

goose-down morphed to goose-step
and the organ grinder ground a different
tune—*Deutschland über alles*—
After she fled, mama stirred her

Goulash in a bowel of grit and when
she died, her ghost departed wordlessly—
the undigested stew inside.

GOULASH

It starts out with the pungent
whiff of onion and bell pepper
braising slowly in a heavy
pot to start the Magyar stew,

a process wanting patience
to enrich the sauce, the garlic's
added half-way through as
well as tablespoons of paprika,

the local flavor blast—pieces
of potato too, then comes a choice
of chicken parts, perhaps some
veal or *wurst*—whatever

variation on this dish. the air's
suffused with haze of steam
rising from *Goulash* as it
bubbled in Vienna years ago.

Today we eat from mama's
blue-and-white glazed Danube
dishes with the silver spoons
we packed to feel at home.

MALAKOFF TORTE

She smooths a stratum of *Schlag*
over layers of coffee-soaked
ladyfingers fixed with a mortar
of rum buttercream in a biscuit
fence erected 'round the pain
mama buried in her *Malakoff*.

Today, guttering candles warm
our buffet of *Liptauer Käse* and
Mayonnaise Eier laid out upon
a crocheted cloth staged with
crystal teardrops, all centered
on the *Torte*, her recipe handed
down with the pan.

MAYBE HE SOLD BOTH

They say he had a good *Schmooze*,
easy banter, lots of friends—that was
then. How did this gift serve papa now,
when his tongue-English no longer

matched his body-English. Always
'his own boss' and so he had to
figure out a way to score that golden
meet-and-greet. No idea with whom

he nattered, didn't matter where he
found that clutch o' goods to scratch
a couple bucks, put *Kartoffel* on the
board, how he trolled to hawk a rack

of neckties on the street. He'd rub
the silk between his fingers like it was
Rumpelstiltskin gold—my sister Peggy
claims it was *umbrellas* that he sold.

NEEDLETRADES

Trying to resurrect the true image of my parents, I sought whole cloth
to fashion patterns larger than shadows cast by figures bearing offerings
of life and words that sheared my heart—but in truth found only
remnants which I stitched into a ghost and scarecrow tied with tooth
and gut.

My father was a cutter of piece goods stacked in three-inch layers on
a table—my mother sewed the seams on power machines—this I recall:
his severed fingertip and her nail pierced with stitches, stopping
for ten minutes with a bloody curse and bandages the whine and roar—
the mad attempt to piece together lives destroyed by war.

TANNERSVILLE

Lakeside—on a log at the rim
of a waterfall that fed a stream,
life rippled on. Papa taught me
to swim out to the wooden raft,

to love the berries in the meadow,
raspberries and huckleberries but,
the strawberries he mused, could
not compare with those from the

Vienna woods, *Walderdbeeren*
of sacred memory. He whiffed them
still, rocking on the porch of a white
boarding house in Tannersville,

a triumph of some measure for
this refugee who only years before
had hawked umbrellas on the street—
now manufacturer of children's

wear grousing that his daughter's
egg was boiled too rare. He was
mine back then, before new little
sister changed the flow. I nursed

my solitude upon a brookside rock,
solarium of tiger lily, wild rose,
honeybee, where musings bubbled
like cold water through my toes.

RADETZKY MARCH

Each New Year's Day I turn my TV to the
concert at Vienna's glittering *Musikverein*
to hear their Philharmonic led by maestros
playing musical nostalgia in that venerable
hall—*Blaue Donau; Vilja Lied; Wien, Wien,
nur Du allein—Strauß* or Lehár, mostly
in three-quarter-time.

When my mother danced she'd twirl me
clockwise, counter-clockwise on the carpet
in our living room, recall the ballroom
floor she whirled upon before they smashed
the windows of our temple hall. Nowadays
they play *Radetzky March* "de-Nazified"
for the accustomed curtain call.

LAST BOAT TO HAVANA

My grandparents, still hidden from the SS
in Vienna's Jewish part of town, held their
breath for cash and visa stamps. There must
have been some lamb's blood on the doorpost
of their home as that global go-between—
the Angel of Death left them alone, didn't

knock—passed over. Dreading doom, they
crossed the Pyrenees to Lisbon among throngs
who sieged the pier for that last boat to Havana,
where they lingered for a year awaiting entry
to the Promised Land. Visa finally in hand—
they exhaled in our living room.

GRANDFATHER'S SEDER

Passover memories slip away. My grandpa's
cadence shimmering the scenes out of our
Viennese *Haggadah*, his retelling of the Jews'
ordeals, their mass migration—our chronicle.

I hear the timbre of his voice, see his *Tallis*—
black bands on ivory with golden appliqué
arrayed around the collar of his suit. He signals
time to raise the glass, to count the plagues.

We dip our fingers, stain our plates with purple
drops, one for each affliction, taste the liquid
of that ancient crop—sweet upon our tongues.
I still sip from his *Kiddush* cup.

THE WANDERING

At sundown
I dipped a spray of wild mint
into the blood of a lamb slaughtered with
a sharp blade (as commanded)

and with this sacred brush
I daubed the doorframe of my house,
the top and sides,
observing an ancient edict of magic and awesome powers
to guard against the perils of the impending hours.

In an oven I roasted a young lamb
seasoned with the salt of tears
and called my family and friends to the table
for a last supper together.

We ate our meal, robed and belted
ready to depart from this,
the land of our oppressors.

When the last bits, the fat and scraps were gone
we sat—bowed in prayer
until the shouts of night subsided
with the light.

As the sun rose (but not our bread)
we left in haste
taking with us the bitter taste of angst
inflicted by a brutal foe

loath to let us go—
to live,
to keep alive the memory of our name.

Our crossing—
a multi-generational migration of deviations
from the straight path
to the final destination continued
over the face of the earth,

for the seeds of our wandering were sown with Moses,
and our journey, of many legs,
as well as countless travails
is seared into the sinews of our descendants.

It is many decades since I've reached the Promised Land.
Now we gather 'round the table in Seattle
while the full moon shimmers on the Sound.

I point to the shank bone
and recall supper
on that last sad day in my old Vienna home
as my grandchild asks

What is the meaning of this?

SONG SUNG TO OMAMA—*Kommt ein Vogel geflogen*

Kommt ein Vogel geflogen
A bird comes flying
your longing soars toward me,
Omama, hovering as you were
in the shadowy rooms of Leopoldstadt,

setzt sich nieder auf mein Fuß
she alights upon my foot
like illusionary feathers. You conjured
my pathways in your missive, guiding me
with the buoyancy of words, while

hat ein Briefchen im Schnabel
with a note in her beak
you dreamt of pulling on my shoes,
as you finally did while I slept in Elmhurst,
understanding the power of

von der Omama einen Gruß
salutations from grandma
your legacy—stand firm, walk
with wonder in the fields that Hakadosh
Baruch Hu provides and by the way—

lieber Vogel fliege weiter
dearest bird fly on
you have your grandpa's eyes. Soar—
over Alpine scarps, grandma,
and the Atlantic swells, Long Island Sound,

nimm mein Gruß mit und ein Kuss
take my greetings with a kiss
circle 'round the red-brick house
in Queens, white picket fence, sit behind
the open window screen,

denn ich kann Dich nicht begleiten
as I can't flee with you
you will have to linger for
a while yet in that room on Rembrandtstrasse
waiting

weil ich hier bleiben muss
for I must remain
until the double-headed eagle none of us
foresaw alights with visa seals clutched tightly
in each claw.

BEDS

Newborn sister, Peggy, had a round, pink
face amid her swaddling on the bedspread.
I was told to keep an eye on her by mama
in that salt n' pepper suit she'd worn six

years before when she had disembarked
the SS Rex without a *Groschen* in the pocket
of that chic *Kostum* created in our fashion
house seized with Hitler's dictum *Juden raus!*

Daddy had been ousted to a room on Britton
and my grandparents—ransomed from the
Cubans by a visa ploy, took over our master
bedroom while mama and I occupied the

large back hall—my sister's crib against
the window wall. When grandpa got the
unmentionable C, aunt Fridl hightailed in
from Africa with cousin Phyllis, littler

than me. Don't know where all they put their heads—
I was sent to stay with daddy's kin—silver-haired
aunt Elsie taught me prayers that carried
me through nights on sundry beds, *Müde*

bin Ich gehe zur Ruh and the *Shema* for
grandpa as he lay there dead. Uncle Martin,
big-shot actor fleeing brownshirts turned up
too. He occupied the speckled maroon

couch, head propped upon his elbow as
he slept—one eye open like a character in
some uncanny *Buehnen* play, the staging
of a creepy war drama in our foyer.

REFLECTIONS

There's a photo of me, about eight,
posing in the courtyard underneath
the kitchen window wearing my mint
green and pink striped pinafore,

blowing bubbles in a ray of sun.
I'm standing there before a cherry
tree, a plum beside the backyard
fence gone long ago. Rainbows

weren't often found beneath those
casements as the shadows traced
the grass. What was it all we had
to do before the bubbles from that

frail pipe popped as family arrived,
then faded from behind the glass
as they moved off to other lives,
smiles fixed in a couple photographs.

epigenetic grit—"it's in my bones"

PHOTO OP

The tatty pockets of my too-short camel
coat—the rough abraded stiffness of it's
threadbare nap, a cast-off thing from

lives of kids who'd worn it new.
At age five, I felt worthy of my papa's
wish to keep that sunny morning by the

schoolyard fence alive, facing his Zeiss-
Ikon brought from Vienna in a crate
along with patterned plates, cooking pots,

goose-down quilts and other stuff they
wouldn't leave behind: a photo album
of a toddler in a lacey dress—not this

shabby kid with memories of flight
from gaslit streets and cobbled lies,
rants of *Wienerblut* and *Juden raus*, so

there I stand preserved in black and white,
a new world radiance behind my eyes that
this chance photo op will not belie.

LUKE BOW AND ME, 1943

At my school in Elmhurst, PS 89, they lined us up
in rows, tall kids in back, short ones in front, where
I stood in my worn second-hand coat beside the other
refugee kid—Luke. English jangled odd to me back
then, but milk n' crackers lulled me home again.

Miss Bubenik, our first grade teacher fixed a giant
sheet of paper to the wall. She chose Luke Bow
and me to paint a mural. We six-year-olds got known
to be the finest artists in the class. Other kids were
asking us to draw their pictures—we kicked artist ass.

I made a carousel with pointy roof of red and white
swirls, glitzy steeds and gryphons bearing riders,
girls in polka-dotted skirts and boys in checkered
shirts with red-and-green striped socks, some kids'
hair brown and curly, others gold and straight,

my white-haired terrier was in the scene and if you
listened you could hear the braying of *Calliope*
lure kids like me with memories of spinning mirrors
flashing off my toddler brain—that was Vienna's
Ringelspiel, merry-go-round I'd never ride again.

Luke painted beasts from earthy tangles of his
Chinese zoo, elephants that lumbered trunk
to tail, orange cats striped white n' black, monkeys
flashing buttocks for their oglers' delight, tile-necked
giraffes and pandas buried in bamboo. We kids

brought old and new stuff to the board—hurled
into a world where sounds were scrambled as our
eggs, the *Dim Sum* or *Shnitzel* truth stuck in our
gut like genetic glue.

ÉCLAIR'S

Our Nazi-fractured German speaking
coterie of friends and family gobbled
chocolate-drenched *Mohrenkopf mit
Schlag* and Schlock at Éclair's on

West Seventy-Second in New York,
a sort of Viennese Café transplanted
to the USA where they would while
away the afternoon with somber and

nostalgic talk of old Vienna's social
scene, that legendary opera house, the
folks whom they sipped coffee with
back then, those who perished, where

exactly were they sent, *Buchenwald* or
Birkenau—and when. They might pinpoint
the day Aunt Fritzi disappeared and how
it was they didn't know, followed by

four seconds of a secret *Yisgadal* inside
the lower gut, synched to guilty gratitude
for some unuttered close escape—and for
the chocolate covered *Mohrenkopf.*

IT'S THE ART

Boobs and belly—fecund female under glass—
that celebrated Willendorf I learned about from
images they flashed on screen in high school class
where I found this Brueghel chronicle as well—

the swirling Tower of Babylon, ancient prototype
for New York's Guggenheim fracturing the sky
over a medieval town on desert dunes teeming with
construction hands like teams of Disney worker ants.

I glimpsed Correggio's submission of the goddess
Io melting in the arms of Jupiter disguised as cloud—
its modern counterpart, *The Kiss* by Klimt, her face
ecstatic, his covert, both swathed in scintillating

folds embracing on a field of gentian and gold.
Such things imbue a glow in memories of Viennese
museums with their chandeliers and agate floors.
But war's wedged mutely in our psyches like

cud stuck in the collective gut. Our beans and
carrots ripened in our Victory Gardens and the
air-raid wardens' hollers disappeared along with
fear of U-boats swarming in Long Island Sound.

I attended fine art schools and found affinity
for paint and ink, pored over images in scores of
slides and fixed to see those noted objects that
survived unscathed in the city we had fled.

This was a lure for me, a madcap wish to touch
the authenticity. I visited the *Opernhaus*, our
Seitenstettergasse Schul and Demel's where
I wolfed *Melange mit Schlag*. I orbited the *Ring*

to call upon the folks now dwelling in our home,
but above all, I skulked the old museum halls.

IT'S IN MY BONES—TA RAM PA PA
I LOVE TO WALTZ WITH MY MAMA

Mother said the Blue Danube was a muddy river—
mud hides bones. There's a snapshot of me age two
sitting on a white limed ledge, my father beside me
to his waist in water. That was when the bonebreakers
came. We treaded brown current fearing to trample
unmarrowed bones. This river churns through me
like new wine from Grinzing—laps at apple-green
memories in three-quarter time, boils double-helix
eddies uncoiling Strauss at five in the afternoon
with swells of Habsburg coffeehouse *Gemütlichkeit*.

Who were those neighbors? Friends who sprinkled us
with water in the yard when we were kids but learned
nothing about showers, who applauded Uncle Martin
playing Faust on stage as he sold his soul for Marguerite,
but also clapped when Martin rolled to dodge impromptu
kicks and pummels as he shoveled Nazi horse shit off
the street, who greeted us *Grüssgott* each day but
squawked *good riddance Jew* as gangsters wheeled
our things away.

Returning to my Lannerstrasse home after the war,
I tried the bell—an old man shuffled to the door.
*Do you know about the folks who lived here in those
former years?* I asked. *Oh them*, he grinned sardonically
his blue eyes peering to my core—*they croaked
decades ago, ain't none of 'em alive no more.*

ICH KANN DIE FÜSS NET SCHLEPPEN
I Cannot Schlepp My Feet

Fifty years ago I traveled back to see Vienna
with my mother and her sister, my Aunt Fridl.
They grew up there during those inspired
years of Mahler, Klimt and Freud.

So great to think they'd talk about their
memories of times before the war, the
schools and parks where they had waltzed
and wooed or had a secret rendezvous.

We strolled about, sat down for coffee
and a *Gugelhupf mit Schlag* and later dined
at Nordsee fish emporium—their herring dish
was mother's choice. As we walked out

the door her knees collapsed. She barely
made it down the street. *I cannot schlepp my
feet* she bleated for the rest of our time.
Once we left Austria—her feet were fine.

EPIGENETICS

I know it in my gut mama, from those eons
of epic silence—why you've told me nothing
of your childhood in Vienna, that wordless

code I read between—not some brightly
painted picture of those early years in that
enchanting town, but the shame that

you've been storing in the gullies of
a bowel that raged at denigration by
the folks you saw as friends, with whom

you'd shared ice cream—what all you've
swallowed, mama, like a goat stuck behind
a fence whose bleating squealed around

your brain when help never came, as no
one dared transgress the frank morass of
your catastrophe. What are friends for?

That question left you standing at the door
with *Kipferl* or some other offering while
alpine crags of perpetuity lodged undigested

pain into threads of DNA. Survivor's guilt—
like stringy *Goulash*, never goes away.

COUSIN FRANK

Also a Vienna escapee, he tended
goldfish, played the violin, loved
my dad, his Uncle Sam—and grew
up handsome as a man can be.

He climbed that golden ladder,
raised a family and suddenly got
old. At fifty he was eighty-five,
white-haired, wheel-chaired—

and died. May he have been the
victim of some riptide in his DNA?

DER SCHLAG SOLL SIE TREFFEN!

They should die of stroke! he swore
for years, consumed by Nazi ghosts
and our eighteen months in hiding

when he stomached thoughts of
looming doom, his stunned gut-brain
trapped in zig-zag fright, a *Blitz*

perhaps, or slow stoked burn, some
final strike causing his amygdala
to glow like a booted jack o' lantern

storming in the head, like those
that gnarled his bowel for all time—
chronic *Magen Schmerz*, the stomach

pain that plagued him till he died
of stroke—the very curse he called
down over decades on that *Volk*.

TALE FROM THE VIENNA WOODS

Skulking vulpine, amber tail—
        in the woods the vixens wail.
Brown-rimmed halo crowns a ragged moon—
            rugged forestland suffused
                          in gloom.

Where does evil work begin?

Fleetingly on briar-thorn the shimmer
            of a rictus grin   catches hair
and scraps of skin—

shattered mother, barren bride
ravaged by a crow
            and thrown   aside.

I hear the rooster shrieking   *crock-a-too*
  blood is pouring from the shoe
  blood is pouring from the shoe

Boney fingers spread their greeting
   from a coven
                woo the wanderers with gingerbread—
throw children in the oven.

Swaying school bells stalk my dream.
   I hear some sirens but   evade
the searchlight beams.
   Shadow men with pounding feet fly
along a lamplit street—road to nowhere

though way is clear,

the end is fraught with fear.

          Flint-eye squatters occupy the trees
fixed to storm, to rise
   to begin their thundering   flight
screaming   whining
               raptors now discharge into the
skies over rooftop, playfield, schoolyard,
                                up into the piercing light

down into the bogged blight they
speed
               to an abyss where foxes feed.

*Helmet-headed troops unloosed
in the land—the ravens roost.*

  As I awake, a hoary specter snags
       a child. I hear the din—
   her will is strong,   the tale is grim.
The merry widow waltzes to
                       a requiem.
     I know the steps but can't begin.   I'm
                           strangely on the

              outside
looking in.

HISTORY LESSON FOR KIDS

I'm sitting calmly on the toilet five
days before my eighth birthday when
grandma comes bursting through

the door—*Hitler's dead*—she yells
triumphantly as I stare dumbly,
haunted by this sudden movement

of the Lord's finger wiping the wolf's
lair clean of the *Fuhrer's* dregs.
Some say his bones were burned,

some say buried, no word of where.
Remarkably—a Hitler puppet was
exhumed after the war from a corner

of their Antwerp yard by two Jewish
puppet masters who had carved and
garbed it for a parody some years

before. Their name was Oznowicz,
whose son Frank Oz of Yoda fame
unearthed it from his attic to display

in a museum exhibition honoring
his parents' name. I can see a spoof
produced by Oz today—it might be

called *Unite the Blight*, a clattering
of wooden dummies "fine as Muppets"
trooped in twos, arms raised in *Heil*,

a tiki-torch parade of marionettes
strung out on "not being replaced"
with puppets carved by Jews.

PASSING ON MY KEYS

I stood before a bronze-caged window
in New York's DMV the day I turned
eighteen, when the State deemed it OK

for teens to take the wheel. I tracked my
groove on arteries spun out beyond those
roads-for-refugees, to *Hit The Road Jack*

or be *King O' The Road*, to show no moss
upon my rims, to drive beyond the byways
of my vision—rattle n' roll tempo I reckon

traveled by True Americans. I've heard
trippers talk of roots they'd ripped from
soil in Donegal, Djibouti, Berlin, Wuhan,

Togo, Stavanger, Benin—lug nuts fastening
their wheel to the axiom of getting there by
what-so-ever vehicle, radix of the USA.

I'm an old hand with a heavy foot. That day
back at the DMV, last thing on my mind was
passing on the keys. My progeny drive well—

they hug the road, their GPS is clear. This
second generation of Americans has license
to make inroads here.

MY NAME IS AVRASH
—because, yes, every living thing deserves a name—
(from Nickole Brown—"Against Despair: The Kid Goat")

I never got a Hebrew name in our Vienna *Schul*
like other kids—mother uninclined to go for ritual,
father just inclined to go along. The wimpled
sisters of the Rudolfinahaus had christened me

into the Catholic faith. My name is *Erika*, Latin
for *Heather*, Greek *Calluna*—it's a kind of broom
for sweeping clean, perhaps like *Judenrein*—
the scrubbing out of our ancestral epigenes.

For one year and a half we languished in our
smoke-filled rooms, then swept across the Alps
to board the SS Rex for our long awaited trans-
Atlantic cruise. My folks would not articulate

their grief lest the *Dybbuk* rise to foul the air
of their new land. And prayer died too. No hustlin'
Ha Baruch Hu except to curse that fucker who
had braised the stew that cooked the Jews.

A word-poor kindergartener in a world where
sounds flew 'round my head' like puzzlers in a
scene that said *your shoes are old—you're wearin'
greenhorn stuff—your clothes look off-the-boat*.

I was oblivious 'cause no one told me straight
you ain't American enough. When my 'immigrant'
kicked in I'd push my skills and ghost-paint
pictures for the rest, draw their spangled socks

from off their feet. At home we nattered German,
Uncle Martin on the couch hallucinating Nazi thugs—
a *Kinderschrek*, he petrified us kids with hugs.
My great love, grandpa, filled the air with

Tauber on the gramophone, walked me to
my Sunday school till illness cut him down.
The night of *Shiva*, when they crouch on
stools to grieve the dead, I was sent to stay

with daddy's kin, got to know aunt Elsie—
hair as platinum as mine is now. She taught
me how to pray the *Sh'ma* and *Müde bin
ich geh zur Ruh* as grandpa vanished,

twice reborn in men who gifted me with
progeny named—*Z'viah* and *Shmuel*—
a birthright *HaKadosh* gives all creatures,
one I'd purloin for myself out of a Hebrew

lexicon—*Avrash*—a word for broom,
like the sound of wind sweeping heather.

ACKNOWLEDGMENTS

PLEA TO PARENTS FLEEING THE WAR ZONE WITH A SMALL CHILD
Bracken Magazine Special Publication Series: *Over Tea and Tears—For Ukraine*, Oct. 2022

RUDOLFINERHAUS, DÖBLING   *Hole In The Head Review* No. 3, Issue 3, Aug. 2022

SMOKE GETS IN YOUR LUNGS   Anthology: *Wingless Dreamer, War Scars In My Heart*   May, 2022

MY GRANDFATHER THE WATCHMAKER CAME AND WENT   *The Winter Anthology*, Vol. 7, 2017

WHAT HAPPENED TO JEKI? OR DOG AS METAPHOR OF WAR   *Connecticut River Review*, Aug. 2023

NEEDLETRADES   *The Far Field*, Kathleen Flenniken, ed., Oct. 14, 2013, reprinted from *Cascade, Journal of the Northwest Poets Association*

WANDERING   *Poetica Magazine*, 2006

IT'S IN MY BONES—TA RAM PA PA, I LOVE TO WALTZ WITH MY MAMA   *Hole In The Head Review* No. 3, Issue 3, Aug. 2022

FRANK   *The Write Launch*, July, 2022

TALE FROM THE VIENNA WOODS   *Bracken Magazine*, Issue 1, Mar. 2016

RANDOM ACCESS MEMORY   *The Write Launch*, July, 2022

THE OBJECT OF THESE POEMS

As Kobi Sitt, producer of the 2022 film, The Devil's Confession: The Lost Eichmann Tapes, *has said, "I'm not afraid of the memory, I'm afraid of the forgetfulness."*

Shver tsu zayn a yid—the bittersweet title of a 1920 Sholom Aleichem comedy, resonant to Jews who have wandered their way through historic travails, has become an implicit portion of their epigenetic destiny. It resides in my gut.

This collection arose from a need to address the gist of my family's displacement as refugees, the plight of our having to leave home to flee persecution, to revisit our immigrant aspirations and travails in crafting new lives, and a sense of the fragility of life itself as events abruptly divulged.

Prior to World War II, about 192,000 Jews were living in Austria. Then came the *Anschluss*, annexation of Austria to Germany, resulting in the murder of over 65,000 Austrian Jews by the Nazis. Around 28,000, including my parents with me, managed to escape.

We arrived as refugees in New York on the SS Rex in November, 1939, having hidden from Hitler's henchmen for a year and a half. Since I was then not yet three, many anecdotes on these pages were quarried from memories my parents passed on to me about life in Vienna before and after the *Anschluss*, and about the tribulations of living as Jews under German occupation before our exodus.

Crafting these poems has kindled some of my earliest recollections, challenging me to reach back to days before conscious pictures imprinted themselves on my mind. To create a persuasive chronicle, I relied on scarce songs and stories passed down to me by family as well as on the old, faded photographs from our disarrayed album. Above all, I've attempted to capture the nuanced tang of events that clung to all the Holocaust-scarred people with whom I was close while growing up—the congregation of family and friends who silently understood each other. May these poems give voice to their collective breath.

February, 2024

GRATITUDE

First—to my parents, Frances Goodman and Samuel Guttmann, who carried me across the Atlantic to safety. Then, to the Schorr family—whom I've never met—for sending us work affidavits to assure the US government we would not be a burden on American society. Also to that Austrian official who decided, at his personal merciful whim, to stamp Exit Visas into our passports.

When we arrived in the US, the *Hebrew Immigrant Aid Society* assisted us in settlement and employment. My folks worked hard, raised me and my sister, and succeeded as proud Americans—that sacred refugee narrative.

I give thanks to my great colloquium of reader/friends whose insightful editorial comments and encouragement helped these poems to grow proper wings: David Rigsbee, Eileen Cleary, Charlotte Pence, and Jed Myers. Deep appreciation also to my dear colleagues at *EasySpeak*, the beautiful community of Seattle poets whose support and keen listening have been invaluable: Jed, T Clear, Mary Crane, Ed McMahon, Rosanne Olson, Peggy Barnett, Donna James, David Thornbrugh, Alex Smith, Jeanne Morel, Ra'anan David, Bonnie Wolkenstein and many others who've supported my readings at various venues. And a special thank you, 52nd Street Band, for embracing my actual drumbeats—which are also at the heart of my poetry.

Huge gratitude to my family champions: children—Hillary, Ric, Joshua, Amy, David, Carie, Jerry, Pam, Alan (of blessed memory), Lynn and David Q and grandchildren—Alix, Adam, Jake, Izzie, Maddie, Amelia, Eden, Adrian, Jonas and Aria.

And thanks to Robyn Beresford and Hassie Chase for their devoted care.

Erika Michael was born in Vienna, Austria, and grew up in New York City where she earned a degree in Fine Art at Pratt Institute and an MA in Art History at Hunter College, CUNY. She moved to Seattle in 1966 receiving her Ph.D. in Art History from The University of Washington. She has taught at Trinity University in San Antonio, Oregon State University, and The University of Puget Sound.

Michael has participated in workshops with Carolyn Forché, Thomas Lux, Linda Gregerson, Laure-Anne Bosselaar, Tim Siebles, Major Jackson, and Jeffrey Levine. Her work has appeared in *Poetica Magazine, Cascade, Drash: Northwest Mosaic, Mizmor l'David Anthology, Bracken Magazine, The Winter Anthology, The Institute for Advanced Study Letter, Belletrist Magazine, The Dewdrop, Aletheia Literary Quarterly* (Third Prize Finalist) and elsewhere. In 2019 she won first prize in the *Ekphrastic* Poetry Contest at the Palm Beach Poetry Festival.

www.ingramcontent.com/pod-product-compliance
Lightning Source LLC
Chambersburg PA
CBHW030058170426
43197CB00010B/1575